DETROIT PUBLIC LIBRARY

Knapp Branch Library
13330 Conant
Detroit, MI 48212
DATE DUE

ESTONIA

ESTONIA

THEN & NOW

Prepared by
Geography Department

Lerner Publications Company
Minneapolis

Series editors: Mary M. Rodgers, Tom Streissguth,
    Colleen Sexton
Photo researcher: Bill Kauffmann
Designer: Zachary Marell

Our thanks to the following people for their help in
preparing and checking the text of this book: Dr. Craig
ZumBrunnen, Department of Geography, University of
Washington; Keith Eliot Greenberg; and K. Jaak Roosaare.

Words in **bold** type are listed in a glossary that starts on page 52.

LIBRARY OF CONGRESS CATALOGING-IN-PUBLICATION DATA
    Estonia/prepared by Geography Department, Lerner Publica-
tions Company.
        p.   cm.—(Then & now)
    Includes index.
    Summary: Discusses the history, geography, resources,
politics, ethnography, economics, and future of this Baltic country, annexed by the Soviet Union in 1940 and independent
once again in 1991.
    ISBN 0-8225-2803-7 (lib. bdg.)
    1. Estonia—Juvenile literature. [1. Estonia.] I. Lerner
Publications Company. Geography Dept. II. Series: Then & now
(Minneapolis, Minn.)
DK503.23.E88 1992
914.7'41—dc20   91-44932
                                                          CIP
                                                          AC

• CONTENTS •

A vendor cleans mushrooms at an open market in Tallinn, the capital of Estonia.

"We raise this flag as a fighting flag and we declare under it [that] we are building a new Estonia."

Edgar Savisaar
Hirve Park, Tallinn
February 24, 1989

In 1992, the Soviet Union would have celebrated the 75th anniversary of the revolution of 1917. During that revolt, political activists called **Communists** overthrew the czar (ruler) and the government of the **Russian Empire.** The revolution of 1917 was the first step in establishing the 15-member **Union of Soviet Socialist Republics (USSR).**

The Soviet Union stretched from eastern Europe across northern Asia and contained nearly 300 million people. Within this vast nation, the Communist government guaranteed housing, education, health care, and lifetime employment. Communist leaders told farmers and factory workers that Soviet citizens owned all property in common. The new nation quickly **industrialized,** meaning it built many new factories and upgraded existing ones. It also modernized and enlarged its farms. In addition, the USSR created a huge, well-equipped military force that allowed it to become one of the most powerful nations in the world.

In 1989, Estonians joined hands to form a human chain that stretched across their land and into the neighboring Baltic republics of Latvia and Lithuania. The 400-mile (644-kilometer) link symbolized the solidarity of the three Baltic States in their bid for freedom from Soviet control.

Young Estonians play on a jungle gym at a day-care center near Tallinn.

Farmers show off ripe cabbages that they harvested from a private field. Until very recently, the central Soviet government owned most farmland.

By the early 1990s, the Soviet Union was in a period of rapid change and turmoil. The central government had mismanaged the economy, which was failing to provide goods. To control the various ethnic groups within the USSR, the Communists had long restricted many freedoms. People throughout the vast nation were dissatisfied.

Several republics were seeking independence from Soviet rule—a development that worried some old-style Communist leaders. In August 1991, these conservative Communists tried to use Soviet military power to overthrow the nation's president. Their effort failed and hastened the breakup of the USSR.

Estonia was one of the first republics to break away from the Soviet Union. Soviet authorities had

Flower stalls are a common sight throughout Estonia, where bouquets are often given as gifts on birthdays and at other celebrations.

annexed (taken over) Estonia, a small independent nation in north central Europe, in 1940. Estonians considered this action illegal and never gave up hope that one day they would again govern themselves.

In 1989, at Hirve Park in the Estonian capital of Tallinn, Estonian activists announced the re-emergence of a free Estonia. A year later, Estonia's leaders worked to establish an economy free of Soviet control. In 1991, following the failed attempt to overthrow the Soviet president, the government of Estonia declared that it had regained full independence. Within weeks, Estonia was welcomed into the **United Nations** as a free and self-governing country.

CHAPTER ONE

The Land and People of Estonia

A t the end of **Kalevipoeg** (Son of Kalev), Estonia's great epic story, the warrior-hero has lost his legs and is chained to the gates of hell. Not yet ready to give up, he vows, "One day...the son of Kalev will come home to build Estonia's life anew."

To Estonians, *Kalevipoeg* is more than just a national folktale. The son of Kalev's condition has long seemed to reflect Estonia's frustration with its status as a captive nation. Since the 12th century A.D., one foreign group after another—Germans, Danes, Swedes, Poles, and Russians—has occupied Estonia. Yet, like the warrior-hero in *Kalevipoeg*, Estonians have never given up the dream of being free and independent.

Wearing the Estonian national costume, dancers perform and sing at an outdoor festival.

Modern clothing appeals to the Estonians who live in Kuressaare, a seaside resort on Saaremaa Island. Saaremaa is the largest of many Estonian islands that lie in the Baltic Sea off the nation's western coast.

Golden foliage frames one of the sculptures in Tallinn's Kadriorg Park, which the Russian ruler Peter the Great established for his wife in the early 1700s.

• The Lay of the Land •

Estonia covers 17,413 square miles (45,100 square kilometers) of land in north central Europe. This area is about half the size of Maine or of Portugal. The nation has coasts on the Baltic Sea, the Gulf of Finland, and the Gulf of Riga—all of which are arms of the North Atlantic Ocean. Estonian territory also includes more than 800 islands in the Baltic Sea. The largest of these islands are Saaremaa, Hiiumaa, Muhu, and Vormsi.

To the east of Estonia is Russia. Across the Baltic Sea to the west is Sweden, and Finland lies to the north beyond the Gulf of Finland. South of Estonia is Latvia, another former Soviet republic that borders the Baltic Sea. Estonia, Latvia, and a third former Soviet republic named Lithuania are together called the **Baltic States.**

The sun sets over one of Estonia's many inland lakes.

Estonia is part of the low-lying East European Plain, which stretches across north central Europe. Estonia's highest point—Suur Munamägi in the southeast—reaches 1,040 feet (317 meters) above sea level. The peak sits on the elevated Haanja Plateau. **Glaciers** (slow-moving masses of ice) shaped this plateau as well as the 550-foot (168-meter) Pandivere Plateau in north central Estonia and the Otepää Plateau in the southeast.

• Waterways and Climate •

Lake Peipsi defines much of the border between Estonia and Russia. For centuries, the barrier of Lake Peipsi prevented migration and lessened the influence of Slavic Russian culture in non-Slavic Estonia.

The largest lake within Estonia is Lake Võrts-Järv, which is connected to Lake Peipsi by the Emajõgi River. Other important waterways in Estonia are the Narva River, the Pärnu River, the Kasari River, and the Jägala River. The Narva links Lake Peipsi to the Narvskoye Reservoir. Most of these rivers freeze in winter, blocking barges and ferries and forcing merchants to send their goods by road, rail, or air.

In general, Estonia has a mild climate. The average daytime temperature in July, the warmest month, is 62° F (17° C). The typical daily reading in February, the coldest month, is 23° F (–5° C). The Baltic islands and western coastal cities, such as Pärnu, are slightly warmer than these averages because of warm winds that blow in from the Baltic Sea. Annual rainfall throughout Estonia is about 24 inches (61 centimeters).

Because Estonia is so far north, it experiences long periods of daylight in summer (June to August), when the northern half of the earth tilts toward the sun. On some days, daylight lasts 18 to 20 hours.

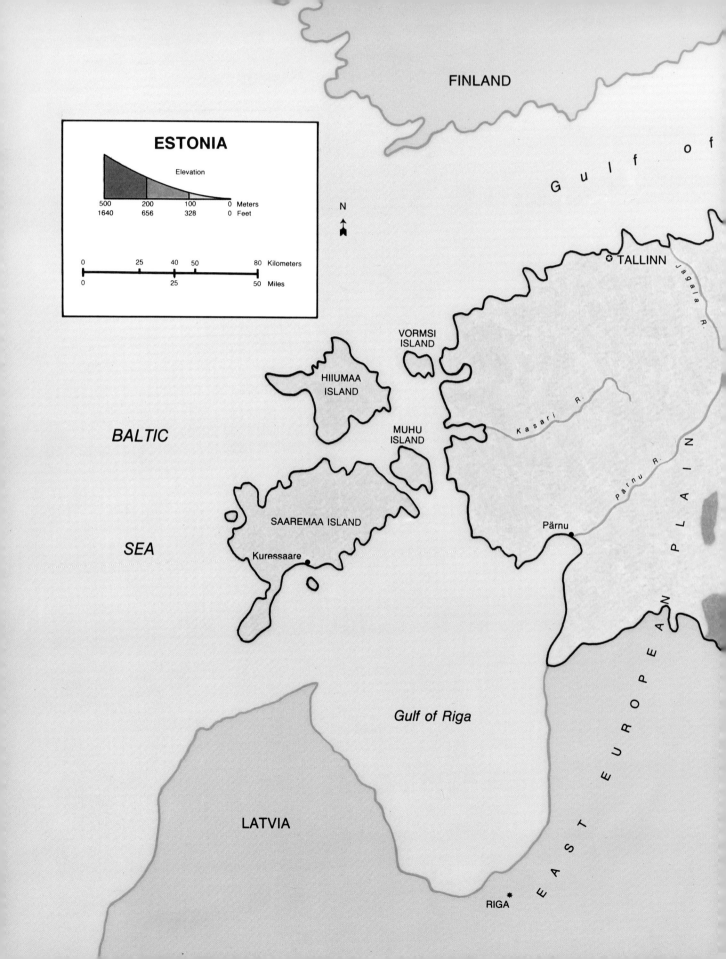

FINLAND

Gulf of

ESTONIA

Elevation

| 500 | 200 | 100 | 0 | Meters |
| 1640 | 656 | 328 | 0 | Feet |

| 0 | 25 | 40 | 50 | 80 | Kilometers |
| 0 | | 25 | | 50 | Miles |

N

✪ TALLINN

Jagala R.

VORMSI
ISLAND

HIIUMAA
ISLAND

Kasari R.

MUHU
ISLAND

BALTIC

Pärnu R.

SAAREMAA ISLAND

SEA

Kuressaare

Pärnu

P L A I N

Gulf of Riga

E U R O P E A N

LATVIA

E A S T

RIGA

F i n l a n d

* St. Petersburg

Kohtla-Järve ●   ● Narva

Pandivere
Plateau

Narva R.

Narvskoye
Reservoir

Lake

Peipsi

RUSSIA

E m a j o g i   R.

Lake
Võrts-Järv

● Tartu

Otepää
Plateau

Haanja
Suur Munamägi ◇   Plateau

LATVIA

USSR

ESTONIA

Bundled up against cool temperatures, schoolchildren walk home from their classes.

Equally long periods of darkness occur in winter (November to April), when the Northern Hemisphere angles away from the sun.

In summer, a light jacket or raincoat is enough protection from the season's cool temperatures and occasional rain. In winter, people must wear coats, gloves, hats, scarves, and boots to stay warm.

• Cities •

Roughly 70 percent of Estonia's 1.6 million people live in urban areas. The nation contains several well-preserved ancient cities and towns, as well as industrial hubs and tourist resorts. The central districts of Estonia's two main cities—Tallinn, the capital, and Tartu—have changed little despite hundreds of years of invasion, occupation, warfare, and turmoil.

The name **Tallinn**—*which comes from Danish words that mean "Danish Castle"—refers to the city's early history as a stronghold of Denmark.*

Pikk (Tall) Hermann, a watchtower in Tallinn's ancient city wall, now flies the national flag of Estonia.

Located on the Gulf of Finland, Tallinn (population 482,000) is Estonia's largest city and busiest seaport. Factories in the capital produce industrial machinery, textiles, and paper goods. Among the city's landmarks are its cathedral, which dates to the early 1200s, and Hirve Park, where many pro-independence demonstrations have taken place. Pikk Hermann, a tall stone tower on Toompea Hill, now flies the Estonian national flag.

In the 13th century, invaders from Denmark founded Tallinn on the site of a small Estonian settlement. The defensive stronghold that the Danes built on Toompea Hill still stands. Later invaders added churches, squares, and cobblestone streets. These features have survived Estonia's turbulent history and have given Tallinn the appearance of an old European city.

Billboards along a street in Tallinn suggest the capital's strong links to the modern culture of Europe.

A young Estonian practices her dressage (horseriding) skills at a fairground in Tartu.

Sitting on the banks of the Emajõgi River in eastern Estonia, Tartu (population 115,000) is the country's educational and cultural hub. The Swedish king Gustavus Adolphus II established Tartu University in 1632, when Estonia was a Swedish holding. Tartu is also home to several other institutions of higher learning. Residents of the historic city, which dates from about A.D. 1030, produce leather goods, wood products, tools, and textiles.

Friends greet each other through an ornate doorway in Pärnu, a seaside town in southwestern Estonia.

The industrial cities of Narva and Kohtla-Järve, both of which lie in northeastern Estonia, have large Russian populations. Narva (population 78,600) is known for its textile industries and power-generating facilities. Kohtla-Järve (population 76,500) is a center for the mining and processing of **oil shale** (a rock from which oil can be extracted).

Pärnu (population 52,600), located in southwestern Estonia on the Gulf of Riga, is a spa and resort that developers built in the 19th century. Seeking to expand their businesses, the developers also constructed a railway to St. Petersburg (a large city in Russia). The overland link brought many visitors to Pärnu throughout the 1900s.

In the early 1990s, Pärnu's future was uncertain. Unrestricted dumping of chemicals and sewage into the Baltic Sea has badly polluted Pärnu's offshore waters. Swimming and fishing are no longer allowed. If cleanup efforts are successful, Pärnu may again become an attractive resort.

Mechanized looms spin colorful fabrics at a factory in Narva, one of the country's industrial hubs.

Cleaning Up the Baltic Sea

For hundreds of years, the Baltic Sea has been a vital trade route and a fertile fishing ground for Estonia and eight other nations that border the waterway. But this valuable arm of the North Atlantic Ocean is in trouble.

People have allowed industrial waste, chemically tainted water from farms, spilled oil, and untreated sewage to pour into the Baltic. These poisonous substances have severely reduced the plant and animal life that lives in the sea's salty waters. The number of Baltic seals, for example, has dropped dramatically because of poisonous chemicals.

The dumping also has affected people. After World War II ended in 1945, the Soviet government threw barrels of chemical weapons into the Baltic. Years later, the chemicals that leaked from the rotting containers killed fish and sickened members of fishing crews.

The Baltic has natural difficulties as well. A shallow body of water with a slow current, the waterway cannot easily flush away or thin out the wastes that flow into it. In addition, large amounts of oxygen-rich fresh water are necessary to support life and to decrease the sea's saltiness. Low levels of rainfall in the Baltic region have reduced the quantity of fresh river water that runs into the sea. As a result, the salt content of the Baltic is on the rise, further endangering the creatures that dwell there.

In 1974, nations bordering the Baltic—including Estonia—met to discuss the sea's future. They agreed to limit dumping and to

Garbage and other debris (above) *line the coast of the Baltic Sea. A glass of the sea's water* (right) *shows the pollution that has resulted from decades of dumping.*

show fishing crews how to avoid the chemical weapons. By the early 1990s, the amount of chemicals leaking into the sea had declined, and oil spills had become rare.

In independent Estonia, environmental groups are working hard to educate citizens about protecting the Baltic Sea. As the lifeline of the nation's trade and home of its fishing industry, the Baltic is vital to Estonia's fragile economy. Free to tackle their own problems directly, Estonians hope they can lead efforts to clean up the Baltic Sea.

• Estonia's Ethnic Heritage •

Humans have lived in Estonia for at least 4,000 years and possibly for as long as 9,000 years. Many theories exist about the original homelands and languages of the nation's first settlers. The Estonian language is much like Finnish and is distantly related to Hungarian. As a result, some scholars believe that Estonians, Finns, and Hungarians originated in central or eastern Europe before dividing and moving to different regions.

Other experts point out similarities between the Estonian language and the Mongolian and Tatar tongues of Asia. The studies of these scholars indicate that Estonians came from the Altai Mountains in southern Siberia (a vast section of Russia that stretches across northern Asia).

Many invaders have passed through Estonia. The most important groups were the Germans, who ruled the country from 1227 to 1561, and the Russians. Estonia was part of the Russian Empire from 1710 to 1918. After a period of independence between 1918 and 1940, Estonia again suffered occupation—this time by the Soviet Union.

Before 1940, nearly 90 percent of the people of Estonia were **ethnic Estonians.** After the Soviet takeover, the Soviets tried to **Russify** the nation. To break up Estonian society, the Soviet government forcibly sent about 100,000 Estonians to other parts of the Soviet Union. At the same time, hundreds of thousands of Russian-speaking people moved or were sent to Estonia, where the Soviet government had promised them housing and good jobs.

Of the 1.6 million people now living in Estonia, 66 percent are ethnic Estonians and 30 percent are **ethnic Russians.** The Russian presence is strongest in the northeastern cities of Narva and Kohtla-Järve, which are geographically close to Russia. The

Some Estonians (top) *sport up-to-date clothing and hairstyles. Other citizens* (bottom) *exhibit the traditional blond hair and blue eyes that reflect their Balto-Finnish ethnic roots.*

Workers at a small, privately owned food-processing plant sort through fresh fish.

remainder of Estonia's population is made up chiefly of Ukrainians, Belarussians, and Finns.

Industrial development—during independence and under the Soviets—has allowed Estonia to achieve one of the highest standards of living among former Soviet republics. Economic reforms that were carried out in the 1970s and 1980s gave Estonia more control of its economy. These changes encouraged productivity and growth.

Estonia's high living standards are also reflected in the nation's health statistics. The average Estonian is likely to live to be 71 years old. This is a lower life expectancy rate than in Sweden and Finland but is about equal to rates in eastern European states. Medical services, which once were provided through a network of state-funded and private hospitals, are now centralized and available to all citizens.

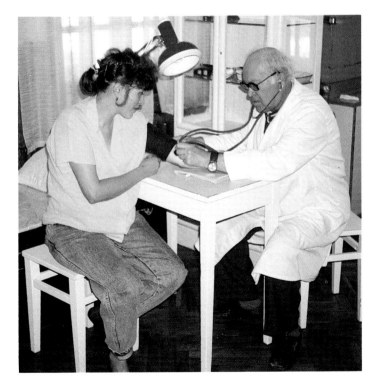

In Pärnu, a doctor takes the blood pressure of a pregnant patient.

A class of 12-year-olds studies math at a school in Tallinn.

A "No Parking" sign appears in both Estonian (top) and Russian (bottom).

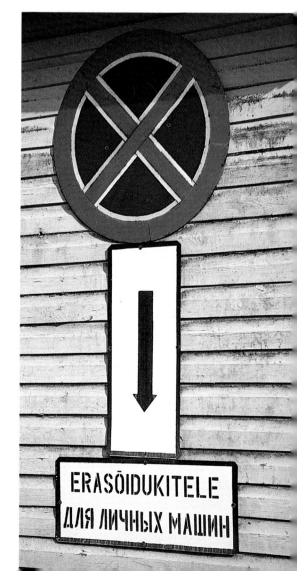

• Language and Education •

By the 5th century A.D., different dialects of the Estonian language were emerging in northern and southern Estonia. The standard dialect of the language is Northern Estonian. Both dialects include words borrowed from German and English and, like German and English, are written in the Latin alphabet.

Russian became Estonia's language of government and law after 1944. Russian uses a completely different lettering system called the Cyrillic alphabet. Although many Estonians—and all schoolchildren—had to study Russian in school, few Russians learned Estonian.

In 1989, Estonian was reinstated as the nation's official language. Russians living in Estonia—many of whom have chosen not to learn Estonian—may find themselves at a disadvantage in seeking jobs and advancement in years to come.

Education has played an important role in the Estonian independence movement. In schools and universities, the culture of Estonia remained alive through the study of the country's traditional literature and history. Under Soviet rule, all education was free. Reforms are now under way in Estonia that may require fees for schooling.

Estonian children are guaranteed an education from preschool through postsecondary studies, which may be at a university or at a job-training center. Primary school takes about nine years to complete, and secondary school lasts two to three years. Tartu University is the country's major institution of higher learning, but Estonia also has schools that teach music, farming, technical skills, and theology.

Once used to house nonreligious Soviet museums, many of Estonia's domed churches are being restored to their former purpose as centers of worship.

• *Religion and Festivals* •

The earliest Estonians practiced a religion that honored the god Taara. The influence of Taara is still evident in a festival held every June 24 to celebrate the longest day of the year. Although Christian traditions changed the holiday's name to St. John's Day, Estonians observe the occasion the way their pre-Christian Taara ancestors did. Dancing, bonfires, and flowers are features of this midsummer celebration.

Most Estonians follow the Lutheran faith, which German rulers introduced in the 1500s. Russian immigrants brought in the Russian Orthodox form of Christianity. Soviet authorities restricted both religions, but believers continued to participate in services whenever possible. Songfests and holiday celebrations remained popular despite the ban on religious practices. These gatherings strengthened Estonia's national identity throughout the decades of Soviet occupation.

CHAPTER TWO

Estonia's Story

Archaeological artifacts reveal that people lived in Estonia as early as 9,000 years ago. Scholars believe, however, that no permanent states existed in the Baltic area for thousands of years. The region's inhabitants lived in small villages and hunted and farmed to support themselves.

Trading did not become a major economic activity until the 9th century A.D. Although most Estonians at that time farmed or raised livestock to survive, the region lay along important commercial routes in northern Europe and on the Baltic Sea. Expanding trade helped Estonians to establish unified communities and to form strong governments.

By A.D. 1000, the people living in Estonia had built a well-organized society that was governed by elected elders. The region was made up of independent counties that occasionally banded together to repel outside invaders or to stage raids on foreign territories.

Cranes rise above the port facilities along Tallinn's seacoast.

• The Coming of Christianity •

Christianity, a faith that took root in northern Europe in the 11th century, arrived in Estonia in the late 12th century. Christian soldiers called **crusaders** had the approval of their leader, the Roman Catholic pope, to wage war against any area that was not Christian. The well-equipped crusaders who attacked Estonia belonged to a German military order called the **Knights of the Sword.**

The knights invaded Estonia in 1193 and met resistance from Estonian farmers. After many bloody battles, the crusaders eventually defeated the farmers, and most of Estonia accepted Christianity. Bishops and other officials of the Roman Catholic Church began to exercise authority in Estonia. Along with the new faith came a group of German landowners who seized farming estates and reduced the Estonian farmers to **serfs** (workers bound to the land).

In the early 13th century, invaders from Denmark occupied northern Estonia and founded the city of Tallinn on the remains of a small trading site. At the same time, the Knights of the Sword still controlled southern Estonia. By 1236, the Knights of the Sword had joined the more powerful **Order of Teutonic Knights.** The Danes sold their Estonian lands to this German order in the mid-1300s. Thereafter, the Teutonic Knights ruled all of Estonia and northern Latvia, a territory that the Germans called **Livonia.**

In the 1500s, a religious movement called the **Protestant Reformation** caused many Germans to turn away from the Roman Catholic Church. The movement spread to the Germans living in Estonia and then to the Estonians themselves. By 1522, many Estonians had accepted the Lutheran faith, which was named after Martin Luther, a German leader of the Protestant Reformation.

A member of the religious Order of Teutonic Knights holds the group's red-and-white shield. Organized in the 1100s, the knights spent decades converting the people of Estonia to the Roman Catholic faith.

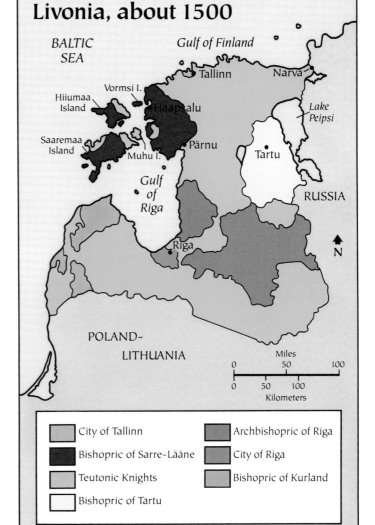

Catholic leaders and the Teutonic order held Estonia and northern Latvia — together called Livonia — in the 1500s.

• New Conquerors •

During the 16th century, the German rulers of Livonia were contending with two powerful and aggressive neighbors. The duchy (dukedom) of Moscow, which ruled lands in Russia to the east, had long been trying to expand into the Baltic region. The kingdom of Poland, which lay to the southwest, was also attempting to annex Livonia.

These powers—as well as others in northern Europe—fought over Livonia and its strategically placed ports. The forces of Ivan the Terrible, the leader of Russia, challenged German control of eastern and central Livonia in 1558. The Russians won, driving the Germans from the region. But northern Livonia sought protection from Sweden, and Poland absorbed southern Livonia.

Conflicts over Estonia continued until the early 1600s. At that time, the Swedes and the Poles joined forces to expel the Russians from Estonia. These two victorious powers then combined their Estonian lands through marriage. By 1625, the Swedish king Gustavus Adolphus II controlled all of Estonia.

Although Estonia was part of the Swedish kingdom, farming estates in Estonia still belonged to

Throughout the 1600s, most Estonians lived in rural areas and worked on large farming estates that belonged to rich landowners.

Through marriage, the Swedish king Gustavus Adolphus II (on horseback) *acquired all of Estonia in the early 17th century.*

members of the German nobility. Their ancestors had been in the country since the 1200s. Most Estonians were landless **peasants** who owed the landowner their labor and a percentage of the crops they produced.

• *Russian Rule* •

Throughout these years of political change and conflict, Russia never abandoned its goal of conquering Estonia. In the early 1700s, the army of the Russian czar Peter the Great attacked Swedish forces in Estonia. The Russians took Tartu and Narva in 1704, and Tallinn and Pärnu fell in 1710. The Russians then imposed their culture and language on the conquered population.

Swedish forces defeated the invading Russian troops of Peter the Great at Narva in 1700. Within a decade, however, the Russians had conquered Estonia.

*In an illustration from **Kalevipoeg**, the Estonian national epic, the hero is shown in battle. Friedrich Reinhold Kreutzwald collected the material for the story in the 1850s, when the nationalist movement in Estonia was gaining strength.*

After the Russian conquest, little changed for ethnic Estonians. They still had few rights, and most people continued to live on the estates of German nobles. When the Russian government enacted land-reform policies, the German nobles resisted them. In the 1800s, Russian laws gave the peasants more freedom to move and to choose their professions. Schooling became more widespread, and new political and social ideas circulated in urban areas. These changes led to a movement for national independence.

In the early 1900s, the Estonian independence movement gained strength. Meanwhile, Czar Nicholas II was struggling to put down a revolution within Russia and was fighting against Germany in the in-

The vivid, blue cornflower is the national flower of Estonia.

ternational conflict known as World War I (1914–1918).

By 1917, the Russian Revolution was threatening to topple the czar's government, and World War I was draining Russia of soldiers and money. In November of that year, Russian rebels called Communists overthrew the Russian government. Estonia chose this time to declare its independence. The proclamation was made on February 24, 1918. Before other nations could recognize Estonia's independence, however, German forces occupied the country.

The Germans were losing the world war and could not hold on to Estonia. The Russian Communists then stepped in, fighting German troops at Tartu and Narva. The Russians were trying to absorb Estonia into their new state, the Soviet Union. But strong Estonian armed resistance forced the Russian government to recognize Estonia's independence in 1920.

• Estonia on Its Own •

Like many nations with a history of foreign domination, Estonia had a hard time ruling itself. Between 1920 and 1933, the country's elected governments lasted an average of eight months. Konstantin Päts, a leader in Estonia's independence movement, assumed power in 1933. He used his time in office to oversee legislative and constitutional reforms that led to new elections and a new constitution—the third since independence.

After achieving independence in 1920, Estonia established Tallinn as its capital city.

Konstantin Päts (right) *headed Estonia's government at various times between 1921 and 1933. In 1933, he gave himself broad powers to make reforms and by 1938 was elected to the Estonian presidency. In 1940, the Soviet army invaded Estonia and deported Päts to Russia, where he lived until his death in 1956.*

This constitution, written in 1937, stated that Estonia was a democracy governed by a president and a two-house legislature. Land-reform policies enabled the government to buy large holdings from powerful German landowners and to divide the properties among poor Estonian farmers. Schooling and health care became more widely available. The new nation's leaders set about improving a weak economy that was still suffering the effects of war and economic decline.

• *Annexation and World War II* •

Estonia's leaders had little time to put their ideas into place. Events in Europe were endangering world peace. Germany, now under the Nazi leader Adolf Hitler, was again arming itself for war. The Soviet Union, under Joseph Stalin, was intent on extending its territory. Small countries like Estonia became pawns in their power struggles.

In 1939, the Soviet Union and Germany signed the **Molotov-Ribbentrop Pact.** It pledged that neither country would attack or interfere with the other. A secret part of the pact stated that Germany would allow the USSR a free hand in taking over the Baltic States.

In 1940, Soviet troops invaded Estonia, Latvia, and Lithuania. Parts of southern and northeastern Estonia were added to Russia, the largest republic in the Soviet Union. For a time, the Germans kept their pledge not to interfere in the USSR's territorial goals. Other nations did protest the Soviet action, but they were either powerless or unwilling to prevent it.

Within Estonia, resistance to the new, Soviet-supported leadership was strong. To counter this movement, Stalin's government imposed a system of **mass deportations.** On June 13 and 14, 1941, for example, Soviet soldiers removed more than 10,000 Estonians from their homes. The deportees were sent to slave-labor camps in Siberia and to camps in other remote sections of the Soviet Union.

Just one week later, Germany staged a massive invasion, breaking the Molotov-Ribbentrop Pact. At first, Estonians were relieved when the Nazis occupied their country and drove out the Soviets. As World War II continued, some Estonians even fought on the German side. Nazi rule was harsh, however. The Germans arrested thousands of Estonians and sent them to slave-labor camps in Nazi-occupied eastern Europe.

Many nations, including the United States, did not recognize the Soviet takeover of Estonia. As a symbol of this policy, the U.S. Department of State continued to display the blue-black-white Estonian flag (center) *in its offices in Washington, D.C.*

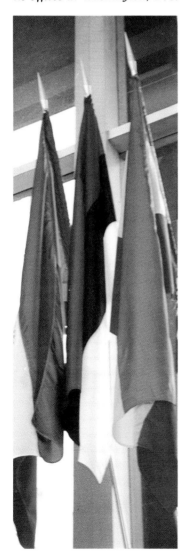

Snow surrounds a monument to the Brethren of the Forest, an Estonian guerrilla group that struck at Soviet army targets during World War II (1939–1945). The Soviets were fighting the Germans, who occupied Estonia between 1941 and 1944.

Near Narva in 1944, Soviet guns shelled the retreating German army.

In 1944, as Germany lost battle after battle, the Soviets returned. Many Estonians were alarmed at the prospect of renewed Soviet occupation. Beginning in 1944, about 100,000 Estonians—or 7 percent of the population—fled to Sweden, Finland, and Germany. Many of the fleeing Estonians drowned when the small boats and rafts used in these escapes overturned in rough waters. Soviet airplanes and submarines sank numerous other refugee vessels.

The Soviets swiftly reestablished their control of Estonia. They called the reconquered land the **Estonian Soviet Socialist Republic (SSR)** and

After the Soviets reoccupied Estonia, Pikk Hermann flew the flag of the Estonian Soviet Socialist Republic—the name the Communist government of the Soviet Union gave to Estonia.

added it to the Soviet Union. The Estonian SSR had its own legislature, which was dominated by Estonian Communists.

After World War II ended in 1945, Soviet authorities scattered many of the remaining Estonians throughout the USSR. In 1949, about 80,000 Estonian farmers were deported to Siberia. The Soviet government seized their farms as part of Stalin's **collective-farm program**, which combined small, private holdings into huge, state-owned farming estates. People from the Soviet republics were brought in to work in Estonian factories and collectives, and the Estonians farmed collectives in other parts of the USSR.

• *Soviet Occupation* •

With many Estonian workers now living outside their homeland, the Soviet government expected the drive for independence to weaken. Throughout the decades after the Soviet takeover, however, Estonians preserved their culture and national identity through songfests, writings, religious gatherings, and traditional festivals. Someday, they hoped, their country would again be an independent state.

The struggle for independence gained momentum in 1985, when Mikhail Gorbachev became leader of the Soviet Union. He began to relax the restrictions on religion, language, and movement within Estonia. On August 23, 1987, thousands of demonstrators gathered in Tallinn to denounce the Molotov-Ribbentrop Pact on its 48th anniversary. In the next year, Estonian activists created the Estonian National Independence party—the first opposition party to form openly in the Soviet Union.

In January 1989, the Estonian legislature passed a law proclaiming Estonian—not Russian—the country's official language. On August 23 of the

In August 1991, conservative Communists tried to take over the Soviet government in a violent coup d'état. During the attempt, Soviet tanks headed for Tallinn's main television studio and stopped news broadcasts. Within days, the coup had failed, and the Soviet central government was in a crisis. This unstable situation gave Estonia an opportunity to declare its independence.

same year, more than one million Baltic people linked hands in a human chain that stretched from Tallinn to Latvia's capital, Riga, to Vilnius, Lithuania—a distance of 400 miles (644 km). Participants demanded that the three Baltic States separate from the Soviet Union.

• *The August 1991 Coup* •

Inspired by the people of the Baltic States, other national groups throughout the USSR began to demand more freedom. In the republics of Ukraine, Georgia, and Armenia, independence demonstrations—once banned by the authorities— became common. Gorbachev came under increasing criticism from fellow Communists who felt he could no longer hold the Soviet Union together.

On August 19, 1991, a group of Soviet military leaders attempted to take over the national government while Gorbachev was on vacation. They ordered the Soviet army to enforce the **coup d'état** (swift takeover) in Moscow, a major Russian city that was also the capital of the Soviet Union. In Estonia, Soviet generals who sided with the coup leaders sent 100 tanks into Tallinn. More than 50 paratroopers stormed the city's television tower to stop broadcast signals.

Designed by prominent national artists, the new Estonian currency—the kroon—carries the pictures of famous Estonians.

Estonia's legislature meets in a pink building on Tallinn's Toompea Hill.

Many ethnic Estonians supported Russia's refusal to allow the military to take over Moscow. Within days, it was clear that the attempted coup had failed. But Russia's brave stand—and the strong support of most Estonians for that stand—signaled great changes for the Soviet Union. Republics throughout the USSR now felt free to assert their national identities, languages, and cultures.

• Estonia's Rebirth •

With the Soviet Union in chaos, Estonian leaders announced the reestablishment of their country's full independence on August 20, 1991. On August 24, Boris Yeltsin, president of Russia, recognized Estonia's declaration. Within a week, 30 nations had established diplomatic relations with the freed Baltic state, and in mid-September Estonia became a member of the United Nations. The Estonian national flag now flies over Pikk Hermann in Tallinn. Estonian stamps and the kroon, the Estonian currency, are replacing Soviet stamps and money within the new nation.

Among Estonia's most pressing concerns are the organizing of national elections and the writing of a new constitution. Political parties—which are free to form—include environmentalists, people who are pro-business, and former Communists.

Tax breaks and other incentives are attracting foreign investors, mostly from Finland, Sweden, the United States, and Germany. Estonians hope that these changes will improve the nation's economy and living standards and will revitalize Estonian culture in the decades to come.

CHAPTER THREE

Making
a Living
in Estonia

E stonia's fine ports have attracted invaders throughout the nation's history. Yet, despite their country's favorable location, Estonians have struggled for economic stability. For many citizens, the next few years are likely to be uncertain, if not just plain hard.

The Estonian government is trying to undo decades of Soviet control over every economic sector. Most Estonians work in factories or on farms, and changes will affect their jobs and income levels. Collective and **state farms**, for example, are being dismantled, and some factories are shifting from state control to private ownership.

On the positive side, Estonia has close ties to Europe and to the United States, which may provide financial and technical aid. The current Estonian government seems willing to make the drastic changes that are necessary to encourage investment and to foster modernization.

*A **private farmer shovels peat**—the decayed vegetation that can be formed into bricks, then dried and burned as fuel.*

• Mining and Energy •

Estonia's most important natural resource is oil shale, a dark, fine-grained rock from which oil can be extracted and refined. Most of Estonia's oil shale lies in the northeast, particularly near Kohtla-Järve. The extracted oil can be converted into gasoline and petrochemicals. Gasoline processed from Estonia's oil shale goes by pipeline to the Russian city of St. Petersburg.

Power plants at Narva use the fuel from oil shale to generate electricity. These plants have been the source of considerable air pollution in past years, and the government is reviewing ways to ease the problem without closing the plants.

Most power-generating facilities are in northeastern Estonia and use both thermal and hydroelectric technology. **Peat**—compact, decayed vegetation that is the first stage of coal—also fuels some stations. Estonia exports some of its electricity to Finland and Russia. The government hopes that electrical power will become an important source of foreign income.

Rocks that contain oil shale pile up at an open-pit mine in northeastern Estonia.

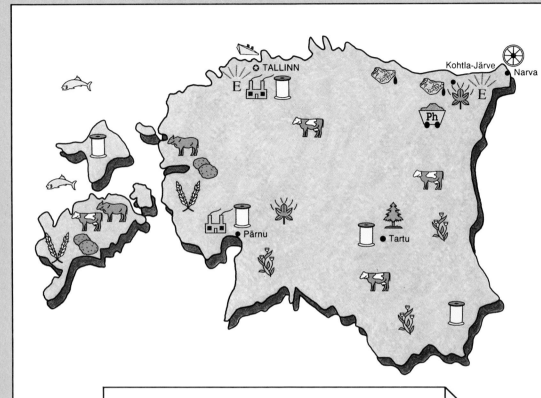

ESTONIA'S ECONOMIC ACTIVITIES

	Industry		Dairy Cattle
	Textiles		Beef Cattle
	Oil Shale		Fishing
	Peat		Grain
	Phosphorite		Potatoes
	Hydroelectric Energy		Flax
	Thermal Energy		Forestry
	Shipbuilding		

Estonia's chemical industry relies on the nation's deposits of **phosphorite**, which can be refined into agricultural fertilizers. The formerly large phosphorite deposits near Tallinn have nearly been exhausted, but substantial supplies of the mineral rock still exist in northeastern Estonia. The government is looking for new methods of mining phosphorite that avoid destroying the environment.

• Agriculture, Forestry, and Fishing •

Estonian authorities are slowly dividing the huge collective and state farms that were set up under Soviet rule. The productivity of these estates had slowly declined since the late 1960s as farming equipment became outdated and as lack of worker motivation negatively affected harvests. The smaller

*A **woman digs up potatoes** in a field near her home.*

Harvesters fill a truck with ripe cabbages.

Thick clumps of birch trees dot the Estonian countryside.

acreages are now being given to individual families in the hope that independent farmers will introduce modern methods and increase crop yields.

The raising of livestock, mainly of beef and dairy cattle, dominates farming in Estonia. The Baltic islands and western Estonia specialize in beef cattle, while the rest of the country is devoted to dairying. Most of the grain used as feed for Estonia's livestock must be imported, and much of the meat is exported. In fact, food products account for more than one-fourth of all Estonian exports. Most milk and dairy products are sold locally. The number of pigs is increasing, in part because they are cheaper to raise than cattle.

Cereal crops, hay, and potatoes are the most important crops grown in Estonia, providing the basis of the country's food-processing and alcohol industries. These crops also supply some feed for livestock. Flax—a flowering herb whose fiber and seed can be spun into fabric—is the main crop in the southern half of Estonia.

Southern Estonia also has sufficient forest reserves to support woodworking industries. In fact, wood is one of the country's few readily available raw materials. Estonia exports about twice as much wood, pulp, and paper as it imports. Nevertheless, most Estonian furniture makers use fiberboard (stiff sheets of wood) to make products quickly and cheaply. Improvements in the quality of wood used to produce furniture could help the wood industry to compete in foreign markets.

Fishing is another Estonian industry with export potential. Catches come mainly from distant parts of the Atlantic Ocean. Much of the haul is sent to nearby former Soviet republics, so that the local market often suffers shortages. Improvements in processing fish could result in this industry's having a better chance of local and global success.

*A **worker** arranges freshly caught sardines on racks for drying.*

• Manufacturing and Trade •

Slightly more than half of Estonia's exports come from the manufacturing sector. As a result, upgrading the nation's industries is a major challenge for the new Estonian government. Many manufacturing facilities were established in the early 1900s. More factories were built after World War II, but outdated equipment and a lack of raw materials have hampered the output of these plants. Many Estonian manufactured goods are of low quality and cannot compete with the products in European markets.

Factories in Tallinn and Narva weave textiles, mostly cotton and linen fabrics. Clothing and footwear are other important consumer items. There are also plants that make precision machinery, lenses and eye equipment, and electronics. Shipbuilding has long been an important part of Tallinn's economy, but a lack of parts, steel, and other materials is slowing production.

The flag of Sweden flies from the newly opened Swedish embassy in Tallinn. Scandinavian nations—such as Finland, Denmark, and Sweden—are likely to become Estonia's major trading partners.

In a textile factory, a worker records the number of new bolts of cloth.

Laborers at this thriving Finnish-Estonian joint venture (economic partnership) produce breaded fishsticks.

Despite the region's problems, foreign businesses are attracted to Estonia, which has a cheap, skilled labor force and convenient ports. Since the late 1980s, Estonia has been involved in many **joint ventures** (partnerships between outsiders and local businesses). Among the 150 joint ventures established in the early 1990s was a huge food-processing plant. These foreign investments offer the possibility of new technology, broader markets, and economic growth.

At the regional level, the three Baltic States may form their own common market to improve trade opportunities between them. Estonia also seeks to establish good commercial relations with former Soviet republics, such as Russia and Ukraine. Trade with these republics is essential, because Estonia needs to buy their fuels, metals, and other raw materials. In addition, Estonian products that are not yet good enough to export might appeal to buyers in the former Soviet republics.

*Economic unity among the Baltic States is a key to their financial survival. Here, **Anatoliss Gorbunovs of Latvia** (left), **Arnold Rüütel of Estonia** (middle), **and Vytautas Landsbergis of Lithuania** (right) sign an accord that pledges their nations to economic and military cooperation.*

CHAPTER FOUR

What's Next for Estonia?

At the forefront of the many changes taking place within and around Estonia are its current leaders. Arnold Rüütel, the president of Estonia, is a popular former Communist who is considered one of the most skilled diplomats in the Baltic region. Prime Minister Tiit Vähi heads a team that seeks to carry out land-reform programs and to resolve ongoing shortages of food and fuel. Another challenge for the new Estonian government is the establishment of citizenship laws in preparation for national legislative elections.

Although Estonia's leaders are enthusiastic about signing trade and diplomatic agreements, the country is not likely to join any new federation of former Soviet republics. Estonians are fearful that a new union will again threaten their independence and culture. The sailors and soldiers remaining on Estonian soil, for example, are symbols of the old Soviet influence that Estonians wish to discard.

*A **sailor** from the old Soviet navy stands along the city wall that overlooks Tallinn. The future of former Soviet naval bases and of other military installations in Estonia has yet to be resolved.*

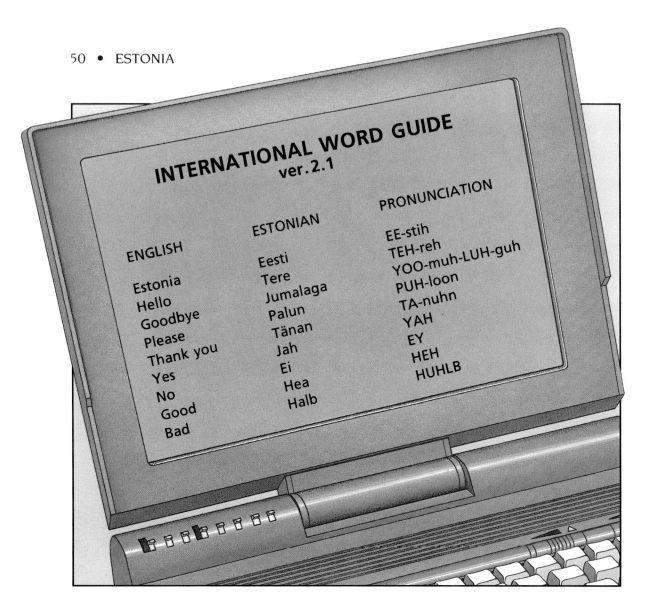

INTERNATIONAL WORD GUIDE
ver.2.1

ENGLISH	ESTONIAN	PRONUNCIATION
Estonia	Eesti	EE-stih
Hello	Tere	TEH-reh
Goodbye	Jumalaga	YOO-muh-LUH-guh
Please	Palun	PUH-loon
Thank you	Tänan	TA-nuhn
Yes	Jah	YAH
No	Ei	EY
Good	Hea	HEH
Bad	Halb	HUHLB

Some observers are worried about the future of Estonia's ethnic Russians, who make up about one-third of the inhabitants of Estonia. The Soviet government transplanted Russian workers to Estonia as part of its attempt to weaken local culture and nationalist feelings.

Many Estonians resent the fact that few Russians living in Estonia have bothered to learn the Estonian language. Ethnic Estonians also strongly oppose ethnic Russians' coming to the country simply for good jobs. Russians—not Estonians—have long managed the biggest industries in Estonia.

The issue has raised the question, "Who is an Estonian citizen?" Some Estonian politicians have said that that right belongs to any resident. Others have proposed granting citizenship only to those who have lived in the country five years, who speak the language, and who are willing to take an oath of loyalty to Estonia. Making the transition from an occupied, victimized territory to an assertive, independent nation is the challenge now faced by the Estonian people and their leaders.

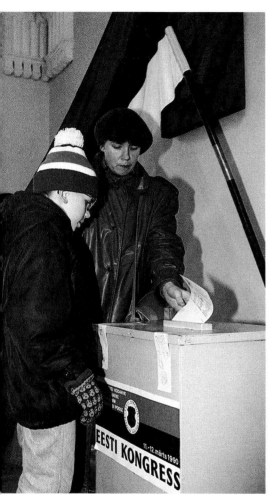

During a national legislative election, a young Estonian watches as his mother slips her ballot into the voting box.

FAST FACTS ABOUT ESTONIA

Total Population	1.6 million
Ethnic Mixture	62 percent Estonian 30 percent Russian 3 percent Ukrainian 2 percent Belarussian 1 percent Finnish
CAPITAL and Major Cities	TALLINN Kohtla-Järve, Pärnu, Tartu
Major Languages	Estonian, Russian
Major Religions	Lutheranism Russian Orthodoxy
Year of inclusion in USSR	1940
Status	Fully independent, sovereign state; member of United Nations since 1991

annex: to add a country or territory to the domain of another nation by force.

Baltic States: a common term for Estonia, Latvia, and Lithuania, all of which are independent republics that border the Baltic Sea in northern Europe.

collective-farm program: a system of large agricultural estates worked by a group. The workers usually received a portion of the farm's harvest as wages. On a Soviet collective farm, the central government owned the land, buildings, and machinery.

Communist: a person who supports Communism—an economic system in which the government owns all farmland and the means of producing goods in factories.

coup d'état: French words meaning "blow to the state" that refer to a swift, sudden overthrow of a government.

crusader: a Christian soldier who waged wars of conquest in the 11th, 12th, and 13th centuries.

Estonian Soviet Socialist Republic (SSR): the name the Soviet government gave to Estonia after annexing the country in 1940.

ethnic Estonian: a person whose ethnic heritage is Balto-Finnish and who speaks Estonian.

ethnic Russian: a person whose ethnic heritage is Slavic and who speaks Russian.

glacier: a large mass of snow and ice that flows slowly across the surface of the earth.

industrialize: to build and modernize factories for the purpose of manufacturing a wide variety of consumer goods and machinery.

joint venture: an economic partnership between a locally owned business and a foreign-owned company.

Hundreds of ethnic Estonians participate in a song and dance festival in Tallinn.

Kalevipoeg: meaning "Son of Kalev" in Estonian, the national epic written by Friedrich Reinhold Kreutzwald in the 1850s.

Knights of the Sword: a German-Christian military order that conquered southern Estonia in the early 1200s.

Livonia: an ancient realm that included Estonia and northern Latvia.

mass deportation: a large-scale, forced movement of people from one place to another.

Molotov-Ribbentrop Pact: a political agreement negotiated by Vyacheslav Molotov of the Soviet Union and Joachim von Ribbentrop of Germany. Signed in 1939, the agreement said that the two nations would not attack one another or interfere with one another's military and political activities. A secret part of the pact stated that Germany would give the USSR a free hand in taking over the Baltic region.

oil shale: a rock from which oil can be recovered through chemical processes.

Order of Teutonic Knights: a German-Christian military organization that took over Estonia in the mid-1300s.

peasant: a small landowner or landless farm worker.

peat: decayed vegetation that has become densely packed down in swamps and bogs. Peat can be cut, dried, and burned as fuel.

phosphorite: a rock that contains phosphate, which may be made into agricultural fertilizers.

Protestant Reformation: a religious movement of the 1500s that sought to reform the Roman Catholic Church.

Russian Empire: a large kingdom that covered present-day Russia as well as areas to the west and south. It existed from roughly the mid-1500s to 1917.

Russify: to make Russian by imposing the Russian language and culture on non-Russian peoples.

serf: a rural worker under the feudal landowning system, which tied people to a farming estate for life. Serfs had few rights and owed their labor and a large portion of their harvest to the landowner.

state farm: a huge agricultural estate owned by the Soviet government but worked by people who receive wages.

Union of Soviet Socialist Republics (USSR): a large nation in eastern Europe and northern Asia that consisted of 15 member-republics. It existed from 1922 to 1991.

United Nations: an international organization formed after World War II whose primary purpose is to promote world peace through discussion and cooperation.

The onion-shaped domes of Tallinn's Alexander Nevsky Cathedral—a Russian Orthodox church—symbolize the Russian Empire's efforts to bring Russian culture into Estonia.

An Estonian gathers fresh tomatoes from a greenhouse behind her home.

• *Photo Acknowledgments* •

Photographs used courtesy of: pp. 1, 12 (left), 16 (right), 23 (right), 35 (left and right), 39, 46 (top), 55, K. Jaak Roosaare; pp. 2, 5, 8 (left and right), 9, 12 (right), 13, 15, 16 (left), 17, 22 (top and bottom), 23 (left), 24 (left and right), 26, 33 (top), 37, 44 (bottom), 45 (top and bottom), Jeff Greenberg; pp. 7, 38 (bottom), 40, 47 (bottom), NOVOSTI / SOVFOTO; pp. 10, 36 (right), 54, © Al Michaud / FPG International; pp. 18 (left), 44 (top), © Shepard Sherbell / SABA; p. 18 (right), © Antonin Kratochvil / DOT; pp. 19, 20 (top), 21 (bottom), 42, TASS / SOVFOTO; p. 25, © Bill Foley / Stock South; pp. 28, 30 (right), Mansell Collection; p. 30 (left), Harlan V. Anderson; p. 31, Historical Pictures Service; p. 32, Richard Sööt; p. 34, Estonian Consulate General; p. 33 (bottom), © Puromies / Lehtikuva Oy / SABA; p. 36 (left), UPI / Bettmann; p. 38 (top), E.T.A. Estonian News Agency; p. 46 (bottom), © B. Bisson / SYGMA; p. 47 (top), Heikki Sarviaho / Lehtikuva Oy / SABA; p. 48, © Robert Blombäck; p. 51 (left), © Markku Ulander / Lehtikuva Oy / SABA; p. 52, © Dieter Blum / Peter Arnold, Inc. Maps and charts: pp. 14-15, 43, J. Michael Roy; pp. 29, 50, 51, Laura Westlund.

Covers: (Front): Yuri Vendelin; (Back): Richard Sööt